TWICE BLESSED:
THE INCREDIBLE AND INSPIRING STORY OF ONE MAN'S ADOPTION,BIRTH MOTHER SEARCH, AND REUNION

TWICE BLESSED:
THE INCREDIBLE AND INSPIRING STORY OF ONE MAN'S ADOPTION, BIRTH MOTHER SEARCH, AND REUNION

BILL SHENOHA

Text Bill Shenoha, with contributions by
Nan Bauroth on behalf of Story Terrace
Design Grade Design, London

First print February 2018

www.StoryTerrace.com

DEDICATION

This book is dedicated in memory of my loving parents, Del and Ray, my birth mother, Marie, and all women who have made the unselfish decision of adoption for their child.

TABLE OF CONTENTS

1

GREATEST GENERATION LOVE MATCH

My grandfather, John Zitz, once hunted moose and elk with Chicago gangster Al Capone. I do know that my grandfather went hunting because I have a wonderful photo of him in the frigid snows of North Dakota standing over a moose he brought down. As to whether the notorious Al Capone accompanied him on that adventure, I can only speculate.

For sure, Prohibition and jazz made Chicago a colorful city during the 1920s, and it was against this backdrop that my parents came of age. My mother, Adel Zitz — known fondly to everyone as "Del" — and my father, Ray Shenoha, were both born in 1922 and grew up during that "roaring" decade in America on the southwest side of Chicago. They were also fortunate to come from upper middle-class families. Ray attended private grammar and high schools, enjoying family and sports activities throughout his younger years. His parents, Bill and Mae Shenoha, along with their extended family, owned several neighborhood butcher and grocery stores that supplied fresh select meat and poultry.

Del's father, John, spent his career in real estate, but he was also an avid outdoorsman, thus his many hunting trips. Given how well he did in real estate, it's possible he had some dealings with Al Capone, but they would all have been on the up and up, for John was a well-respected businessman in Chicago. Interestingly, John also owned a music store. This may have been because, during the late 1920s, Louis Armstrong became one of the most renowned figures in the world of jazz, and Chicago teemed with cabarets where locals could hear some of these jazz greats. The arrival of talking pictures from Hollywood, the "talkies," would also fuel the

Grandfather John, moose hunting in North Dakota

first musical picture. Del's mother, Veronica, was a loving, devoted figure throughout her marriage to John, staying at home to raise their four children.

When Del and Ray reached their teens, they became high school sweethearts, seemingly destined to marry. But the winds of war were blowing, and in early 1942, at the age of only 19, Ray traded in his butcher's knife at the family store to enlist in the U.S. Navy. His basic training was in electrical engineering, and he ultimately served our country on a fleet of submarines in the South Pacific theater of war. In the meantime, Del completed her education at a public high school, and continued living at home with her parents while honing her typing skills, eventually finding a position as a secretary in Chicago.

Like so many Greatest Generation love matches, Del and Ray were forced to carry on their relationship mostly via mail, writing to each other often and snatching a rendezvous whenever they could at various port cities on the west and east coasts. During these turbulent times, they were able to occasionally return to Navy Pier in Chicago where they took advantage of the opportunity to visit together with family and friends. It was during one of these leaves in Chicago that the couple became engaged. They married soon after, in March 1944, spending a long weekend honeymooning in New Orleans before Ray had to return to his duties in the South Pacific and Del resumed her work, living at home with her parents.

When World War II finally ended in 1945, the reunited couple settled into normal married life in a small one-bedroom apartment not far from where they had both grown up. Ray's electrical engineering training in the military served him well, enabling him to find a position with a division of General Motors in the Chicago suburb of La Grange, while Del continued her secretarial career.

BABY BOOM BECKONS

Like so many couples who had put having a family on hold during the war, Del and Ray were anxious to join the baby boom in the first few years of their life back together again. However, for several years, Del had problems becoming pregnant. By 1950, frustrated and anxious over her inability to conceive, they began exploring the option of adoption. Del and Ray were both raised Catholic, and early that year they had met several times with Catholic Charities of Chicago, which had been founded in 1910 as a human services organization counseling families. After much prayer and consideration, Del and Ray made the decision to adopt their first child.

The adoption process, however, raised questions in the minds of the now almost 28-year-old husband and wife. One major concern was the need to move from their small, one-bedroom apartment into a larger home. The financial burden of having a child worried them as well. In the final analysis, though, these issues were minor in comparison to

Mom and Dad's wedding, March 1944

their anticipation of starting a new family.

On November 20, 1950 Del and Ray's dream was realized when a healthy eight-pound, one-ounce baby boy was born at Mercy Hospital in Chicago. The baby, with no choice of his own, was placed for adoption by his mother with Catholic Charities, hopefully to be raised by a loving, two-parent family. Two weeks later, this smiling, healthy baby boy was put into the excited waiting arms of Del and Ray. They would name their new boy William Andrew Shenoha, after Ray's father.

Del and Ray's first Christmas a few weeks later was an exhilarating time for the new family. Little did they know that the season would bring even more joy and surprise, for the young couple shortly learned that Del was pregnant. Ten months after adopting Bill, as they called their son, Del and Ray welcomed a healthy baby girl that they named Mary. The couple who had struggled to start a family for so many years now had "Irish twins," an expression referring to having two children under the age of one.

A GOLDEN CHILDHOOD

This doubling of the family within only a year made the one-bedroom apartment crowded, so in the ensuing months Del and Ray decided to buy a two-story home a short distance away. Del's sister, Dorothy, and her family agreed to live on the first floor, while Del, Ray, and their growing family resided on the second floor. With two young children both

Mom giving me a bath, circa 1951 — no jacuzzi tub?

nearing one year of age, Del's days were now doubly busy, and to complicate matters, Ray was working nights at GM in the early stages of his career. Then, in 1952, tragedy struck when Del's father, John, suddenly passed away at only 60 years of age. The entire family was heartbroken over this unexpected loss.

Del and Ray quickly decided that her widowed mother

Veronica would come and live with them. In addition to providing a home for Veronica, this move would provide another benefit — a helping hand raising the Irish twins, Bill and Mary. The children were already very fond of her, calling her "Nana." In effect, Veronica provided Del and Ray with a full-time babysitter so that Del could resume her career, which she very much desired to do.

Thanks to this change in circumstances, Del was able to spend her next 27 years working outside the home while her mother, Veronica, provided a loving, guiding, and helpful hand bringing up the two children. During the 1960s, Del served as executive secretary to O.W. Wilson, superintendent of police at the Chicago Police Department. Later she worked for Arthur Wirtz, founder of the Wirtz Corporation, who became a powerful figure in sports and arena operations in Chicago. His son, Bill, eventually became principal owner and chairman of the Chicago Blackhawks National Hockey League team.

Once Veronica settled into our family home, my sister Mary and I enjoyed an almost idyllic childhood, growing up in a comfortable environment in southwest Chicago. We both attended private Catholic schools from kindergarten through grade eight that were a short distance away in our neighborhood, which gave us the luxury of walking home every day to have lunch and watch TV with Nana.

In July 1958, my parents received another unexpected bundle of joy with the arrival of a second baby girl they named

Jean. I remember my Dad coming home one day and telling Mary and me that we had a new baby sister. That addition to the family also meant we now had six under one roof. It was shortly after the birth of Jean that my parents shared a brief story with me about my adoption. I was around eight years old, and at that point it seemed just the right time to mention this fact to me. My mother did most of the talking, telling me that I had been this beautiful baby boy who smiled back at them when they were at Catholic Charities one day.

Her story was simple to understand and appreciate at the age of eight, and I didn't think much about it at the time. Mary, Jean, and I all grew up surrounded by loving, caring, and hardworking parents, and our grandmother. I never

My baby sister Jean, me, and my "Irish Twin" Mary at my niece's wedding

felt different in any way. We all were equally loved. All of us received a superb education, and went on to graduate from college, eventually earning our master's degrees. I went to Loras College, a private Catholic college in Dubuque, Iowa, while my sisters went to the University of Illinois.

DARING TO WONDER

In 1973, a year after I graduated from college, I married, and five years later my wife and I were blessed with a healthy baby boy we named Ryan. We were living in the Chicago suburbs, and it was during the first years of Ryan's life that I began having concerns about the possibility of any long-term health issues for both Ryan and myself because I did not know the medical history on my side of the family. My wife and I were well versed in her background, knowing she had healthy parents and siblings, but because I had been adopted, I had no information on my own medical history.

With these general concerns in mind, I began to reach out and search by myself for my birth mother. I was aware that my parents had adopted me at Catholic Charities, so in January of 1979 I called them, curious to see what information they could or would provide me and if they had any medical history of my birth mother. The following month, I received a letter in response to my request stating that my birth mother was a 30-year-old woman of German descent from a small community outside of Chicago. The letter also indicated that she had come to Catholic Charities for reasons of confidentiality.

The letter went on to say that my natural father was a 27-year-old man of Italian descent. "Your mother chose adoption for you so you would have a loving, two-parent family," the letter noted, adding that my birth weight was eight pounds, one-half ounce; the delivery was normal and the family medical history was essentially negative — meaning nothing of consequence. "You were placed with your adoptive family on December 4, 1950." All of this was pretty much new information for me, and it was a start. I had at least found out that there were no major medical complications at the time I was born.

In April 1981, my wife and I were blessed again with a healthy baby girl we named Kerry. Several months after her birth I began once more thinking about potential health concerns, if any, on my side of the family tree. Was I being an overly concerned Dad? Ryan was an active, healthy two-year-old boy. He and Kerry both enjoyed their neighborhood and had many friends on the cul-de-sac where we lived in Naperville, Illinois. There were four boys on our street all born in 1978. It was an enjoyable time for my children, and I was busy with work and our growing family, so I temporarily put my concerns on hold.

Marie, 24 years old

2

MY SEARCH ANGEL

In the fall of 1984, I accepted a sales position with a new company that transferred me to Charlotte, North Carolina the following year. Life grew busy as Ryan, now seven years old, began school. Kerry was four and would soon follow in her brother's footsteps to St. Ann Catholic Grammar School. Over the next few years, I flew to Chicago several times a year for sales meetings and family vacations. On one of my return plane trips back to Charlotte in the summer of 1988, I was catching up on Chicago happenings in the Chicago Tribune newspaper when a posting in the want ads for someone offering help in adoption searches caught my eye.

Intrigued, the next day I called the number listed in the ad and it was at this moment that my journey to find my birth mother would take a giant leap. The man who answered the phone was named Mike Edwards. He had also been adopted, and as a consequence of his own experience tracking down his birth mother, now had a sideline business conducting adoption searches for people for $125 per search. We spoke at length about my reason for searching for my birth mother, but also talked about how fortunate I was to have been adopted and placed with a loving two-parent family and enjoy such a wonderful life and childhood. At the same time, he understood the reasons for my desire to locate my birth mother.

During our initial discussion, I told him about the letter I had received from Catholic Charities in 1979 with the limited information that my birth was normal, my birth mother came from a town outside Chicago, was 30 years old and gave me up for adoption so I could have the benefit of a loving, two-parent family. When I shared the information that I had been born on November 20, 1950, he said that knowing this fact could be a big break in my search. Excited by his positive response, I sent my $125 check the next day hoping Mike's own search experience and others he had conducted for clients would help solve my puzzle.

PAPER CHASE

Several weeks passed. The next time Mike called, he informed me that many of the babies who were adopted from 1948 to 1955 had been listed in the *Law Bulletin*, a weekly publication for Chicago attorneys. Mike said he would start reviewing the microfiche from those years in hopes of pinpointing my adoption notice.

Several weeks later, I received another call from Mike. "We have some good information," he announced, reporting that after searching the records of the *Law Bulletin* around the year of my birth, he had found a notice of my adoption listed in the June 12, 1951 edition. Mike then proceeded to read to me over the phone, "Raymond Shenoha and wife adopt Paul Leroy Ruesken." What's more, the number on my birth certificate matched the listed number on the posting in the *Law Bulletin.*

Incredible as it seemed, I now had a last name associated with my birth mother. Mike then quickly reminded me that the letter from Catholic Charities had stated that she came from the Chicago area. With that information in hand and her name, my mind began swimming with questions: Was my birth mother still alive? If so, was she living in the Chicago area? Where could she be? Many unanswered questions remained, yet I was excited that my search for her was still alive.

In the following days, I spoke with Mike again, and this time he asked me if my parents had ever mentioned an adoption decree, a document legalizing my adoption. He explained that an adoption decree formally creates a parent-child relationship between adoptive parents and the adopted child as though the child were born as the biological child of its parents. I told him that I had never seen or heard of any such adoption decree related to me.

Fortunately, Mike's years of helping other adopted people search for their birth origins had taught him a lot about the inside workings of the Chicago court system. Armed with the information he had found in the *Law Bulletin* and perhaps with a favor from friends in the system, he was hopeful he could help me obtain a copy of my adoption decree.

My search now became like an NCIS plot as Mike outlined exactly what he wanted me to do. Since I was born and grew up in the Chicago area, he directed me to write a letter as if I were my Dad to Judge Joseph Palmer at the Cook County Circuit Court. When he mentioned that name, I paused a moment because it sounded familiar. I had gone to grammar school in Chicago with a Joe Palmer. Could he by chance be the same judge? There was no way to tell. Mike then told me to state in this letter that I (my Dad) had recently moved to North Carolina and during the move misplaced my son's adoption decree, so he would appreciate it if the court could send him a new one. Mike said I should sign my Dad's name to the letter, which made me smile, because years before, I had learned to sign my Dad's name when I had gotten C's on my test grades and didn't want him to see those results!

The next day, I followed Mike's instructions exactly and then mailed my letter to the Circuit Court of Cook County, Illinois. To my surprise, within two weeks I received a letter from the court telling me they would authorize the issuance of a certified copy of my son's adoption decree upon receipt of my check in the amount of $3 payable to the Clerk of the Circuit Court of Cook County, Illinois. I immediately sent the certified check and within two weeks received the promised copy of my adoption decree as well as my certificate of adoption.

At long last, my legal paperwork was in hand. Now that I

knew the name of my birth mother, I began calling directory assistance in Chicago — in those days there was no Internet — trying to locate anyone by the last name of Ruesken. I finally got the name of a Ruesken in Naperville, Illinois, of all places. Before I called, though, I realized I needed to make up a story as to why I was searching for a Ruesken. So when a man answered the phone, I told him that my parents grew up in the same neighborhood with the Ruesken family and were about to have a big anniversary party and wanted to invite them to the reunion. He was very skeptical, obviously puzzled by my questioning and who I said I was. He said he would look into it, but nothing ever came of our conversation.

Meantime, now that Mike had my adoption decree he said he would follow up with more information soon, so I anticipated his next call would have even more exciting news. Instead, I was stunned to receive a letter from him a few weeks later stating that although he had made some progress in my search, he had decided to end his efforts. He said his search business was not making any money because people were defaulting on their payments to him. I immediately called him and reminded him that I had paid the $125 fee, but Mike did not waver, simply saying that he was sorry and wished me good luck in my search. I thanked him for helping me get started. At least he had discovered my family name of Ruesken. However, I was discouraged by this unexpected turn of events, as it seemed I had hit yet another dead end.

9.21.88

Dear Bill:

Since we last talked early last summer – I have made the decision to stop searching for others – as it takes a lot of time and effort and in the long run I end up losing money. —

I have three cases now which are complete where they paid half of my fee and I doubt if I will ever get the rest – which includes my out of pockett expenses as it has been a long time since I billed ~~any~~ of them. And I won't ask again —

So maybe you can understand why I stopped – Anyway I don't know who to tell you to call but I'm sure you will see a way to finish this on your own –

Good luck

Mike

Mike's letter terminating the search

LOST & FOUND

Once I absorbed the shock of losing Mike's help, I regrouped and determined to look around Charlotte for someone like him who could help finish the search. After all, I now had some good, solid information, but no real answers. For weeks I searched newspaper ads, and then by some form of divine grace, in early December 1988, I discovered a company in Charlotte called Adoption Search. The name sounded appropriate to my needs, so I contacted them and once again shared the story about my journey to locate my birth mother.

Adoption Search was owned by Ms. Chris Johnson and Ms. Janis Schneider, who occupied a small office in Charlotte, and were providing the same adoption search assistance as Mike did in Chicago. They told me their fee was $150, so I made an appointment to visit them the next week, where I reviewed all my previously uncovered information, as well as the copy of my adoption decree and certificate. During our discussion they reminded me of something Mike had warned me about earlier — that birth mothers who place their children for adoption often put fake names on the legal documents to protect their identity. Although we could hope Ruesken was my birth mother's real maiden name, it might prove a false lead.

To my amazement, Janis called several weeks later to report that she and Chris were 99 percent certain that they had found my birth mother. The rest would be up to me. They then launched into a conversation to help me prepare for my initial phone call to her. They pointed out that by now my birth mother would be around 68 or 69 years old, might be married, have a husband and perhaps even children still at home, so she might not want to talk to me. Or, she might not answer the phone. They wanted to compose me mentally for what might take place.

I will never forget that day Janis called with the news that she and Chris thought they had found my birth mother. I was sitting at home in my office, and when she told me they were almost sure they had discovered her contact information, I experienced a sudden rush of excitement and joy and wonderment. It had been only a short period of time in which these two women had come up with this critical information, and now it seemed, were about to help me reunite with my birth mother whom I had never met.

At the same time, Janis and Chris were trying to temper my expectations so I would not be disappointed if the phone call did not pan out the way I hoped. They cautioned me that not all attempted reunions with a birth mother were successful, and tried to force me to think about issues I had not considered up to that point. For instance, I had not considered my birth mother's history or how she might feel at getting this call from me. I did realize that it would come as a shock to her after so many years. Although I might be feeling tremendous excitement at my end, I needed to understand how traumatic this call might be for her.

As I listened to what Janis and Chris were advising me, my mind was swirling with emotions. I thought about the fact that I had been adopted, and who had adopted me, and that I had benefited from having two loving parents who had given me such a wonderful life. That I now had two healthy children, and because of my concern for them I had begun this journey that already involved several twists of fate. I rarely read ads, so it was ironic for me to have spotted that small posting in the *Chicago Tribune* and found Mike, whose experience was a perfect fit at that stage of my search. Had I not contacted Mike, God only knows if I would have hit nothing but dead ends and given up my search. At this point, though, I was just overcome by curiosity to connect with my birth mother.

THE PHONE CALL

In the following few days, I spoke with Janis again and she reviewed how she wanted me to speak with my birth mother, whose name was now Marie Ruesken Jones, indicating that she had probably married at some point in time. Janis reminded me how sensitive and upsetting this call could be for both of us. Marie, now in her late sixties, might not want to have anything to do with me. Throughout my adult years, I had heard a few stories of birth mothers who never wanted to reconnect or have a relationship with their child. On the other hand, I had heard some heartwarming stories of enjoyable and satisfying reunions. After turning all of this over in my mind, I was prepared to accept both possibilities. I would respect her decision, but deep down inside I hoped that she would be as thrilled to hear from me as I would be to connect with her.

Janis insisted I carefully consider all the scenarios and call her the next day. I had a restless night, but distinctly recall that for whatever reason I remained positive, excited, and comfortable with placing the call. Perhaps it was because things seemed to have been so divinely guided in my search, and the incredible way that everything had eventually fallen into place. I was more positive than negative because of the direction I felt I had been led.

Once my fears were behind me, Janis gave me the exact wording she recommended I use on the call: "Hello, my name is Bill Shenoha. I realize you may not know me by that name, but I was born November 20, 1950 as Paul Leroy Ruesken and I have reason to believe you are my birth mother. I understand that you may not be able to talk to me at this moment. I am living in Charlotte, North Carolina and my phone number is xxx, and we can talk when you have time." Having this script in front of me made me more relaxed, so I thanked Janis for all her guidance and told her I would make the call the next day.

It was mid-afternoon the following day when I dialed the phone number that Janis had given me. A lady answered, and I asked to speak to Marie Jones. She acknowledged that she was Marie Jones. I then began to read my prepared script. As I finished each sentence, Marie would briefly interject a noncommittal, "OK." When I finished the entire script, she again simply said, "OK." I thanked her and we both hung up the phone.

I distinctly recall there was no excessive expression of excitement in her voice for those few moments we talked, and her lack of response left me feeling empty. Was I to assume she didn't care to speak with me anymore, or was she too busy to talk to me? Were her husband or children in the room allowing her only to say "OK," or did she think my call was a hoax? All these thoughts raced through my mind as I hung up.

Nevertheless, I anxiously waited for her to call me back in the days that followed. And then the weeks. And then the months. After nearly six months of silence since I had placed that fateful call, I decided to try calling Marie again. When I dialed her number this time, however, I received a recorded message saying the phone number had been disconnected and no further information was available.

My immediate reaction was "Oh my God, what happened?" I knew she was in her late sixties. Had she perhaps passed away? Distraught over this possibility, over the next few days I made phone calls in the area to investigate, but no one by her name was identified. I began to feel hopeless, thinking that she simply was not interested in reuniting with her son. As time passed, however, I gradually grew okay with that theory. The fact we had at least spoken, that she realized I was alive and well and not a casualty of the Vietnam War like so many other men my age, gave me a sense of comfort. I spoke with Janis once more, detailing my phone call with Marie and the results. I thanked Janis for all her help and told her I would stay in touch. But in my heart, I was despondent. I had lost my birth mother once, and then found her. Now it seemed, I had lost her again — this time likely forever.

3

LOST, BUT NOT FORGOTTEN

Six years passed. During all that time I never contacted Janis in an attempt to try once more to locate Marie's whereabouts. Perhaps this decision was based on a fear of rejection by my birth mother, although somewhere in my mind I still retained a sense of hope. Instead, my focus during those six years was raising my two children. Ryan would soon graduate from high school and head to North Carolina State University in Raleigh on an academic scholarship and major in engineering. Kerry, 15, was focused on her academics and playing for her school's softball team. It was also during this period in my life that I went through a divorce, and due to that change in circumstances, had moved twice in Charlotte.

January 26, 1996 started as a normal work day. It was cool yet sunny as I was getting settled in my new residence and working from my home office. As I sorted through the day's pile of mail, I suddenly noticed an envelope from Catholic Charities that had been forwarded to me at my new address.

My heart skipped a beat. I didn't know what to expect.

Opening the envelope, I found a letter dated January 22, 1996 from Grace Jackson, a caseworker in the Post Adoption Services Department, informing me that my birth mother Marie Ruesken Jones had contacted the office and asked to be given my phone number and whereabouts. The letter then asked me if I would be willing to write a letter to Catholic Charities and provide my new phone number and send it to their Chicago office to document that information.

To say I was elated would be an understatement. After so many years it seemed God was intervening again and giving me another chance to reunite with my birth mother. I immediately wrote a letter back to Catholic Charities assuring them that yes, I would like Marie to have my phone number so we could further develop our communication. I also noted that I wanted to assure Marie I would respect her privacy and do everything to make her feel comfortable with this situation. Lastly, I asked that Marie call me on January 31 at 8 p.m. EST.

I was so anxious to get my response back that I overnighted my letter to Catholic Charities. I couldn't believe that after six long lost years from when I had first attempted to connect with Marie, that she had wanted to reach out to me. But so many questions now surfaced in my mind. How did Catholic Charities find my new address in Charlotte? I had moved two times since that call to Marie six years prior. And why the six-year gap since our last conversation? These were just several of the questions I longed to have answered after such a long time.

Needless to say, I was impatient all day on January 31

waiting for 8 p.m. to arrive. To my elation the phone rang right on time, and when I answered I began my long-awaited phone conversation with Marie, who by then was 77 years old. We talked for almost two hours that night, and during that discussion the mystery behind the six silent years was finally revealed.

A POCKET FULL OF QUARTERS

Marie had quite a story to tell, for as fate would have it, the past six years it had been her turn to search for me without success. She explained that the problem started during our initial phone call when I read my script and simply stated my name and phone number. Although I had given her my number, I didn't think at the time to ask her to repeat it back to me to be sure she had it correct. As it turned out, in all her excitement at receiving my call out of the blue she had transposed one digit in my phone number.

To compound matters, although I had stated my name in our initial call, in my nervousness at that moment I neglected to spell it for her. So she had hung up the phone without realizing that she not only had the wrong phone number for me, but also no knowledge of the correct spelling of my last name.

As if all that weren't enough to stand in our way, she explained that two months after our initial call she and her husband Bill had moved to Brainerd, Minnesota. Bill began suffering the early stages of congestive heart failure, so they chose to move closer to her brother and the medical care available at Mayo Clinic. This move explained why I had gotten that recorded message about her phone being disconnected with no forwarding information.

Against all these seemingly impossible odds, however, Marie had persevered. Heartsick once she realized she likely had the wrong phone number for me, she remembered I said I lived in Charlotte, North Carolina. Out of desperation she began leaving her house alone at various times of the day with a pocket full of quarters and heading to a nearby payphone where she would call directory assistance in Charlotte. The operator would then ask her how to spell Shenoha but she could only make a best guess, and since she never managed to spell it correctly, the operator always gave her the number of someone else. Whenever she dialed these parties, they would reply that there was no one at that number by the name of Bill Shenoha and hang up on her. This agonizing process went on for six endless years.

DEL'S SECRET GIFT

As the fruitless exercise of dialing wrong numbers and getting hang-ups dragged on, Marie confessed that she began to wonder if my initial call six years before had been a hoax. So in 1996 she finally took a deep breath and called Catholic Charities in Chicago, where she was connected with Grace

Jackson in the Post Adoptive Services Department. Marie explained to Grace that she had received a call from a man claiming to be her birth son six years ago and that he had told her he lived in Charlotte. Marie also told Grace that she must have transposed the phone number he gave her at the time, and tried over and over in the ensuing years to find his correct number, but to no avail.

Marie remarked that at this stage she felt she and Grace must have been touched by an angel. Although Grace was due to retire soon, the more she heard of Marie's story, the more she wanted to help. The problem was that in 1996 the state of Illinois had a closed adoption policy, so vital birth records could not be obtained. Nonetheless, Grace agreed to investigate further to see if she could find the name of my adoptive parents.

Her research proved fruitful. As it happened, my parents Ray and Del had retired and settled in the Phoenix, Arizona area in 1981. Although my father had passed away in 1994, Del had chosen to remain in Arizona, happy with her friends and activities in an active retirement community. Somehow Grace located her address and directed a letter to Del informing her that my birth mother was attempting to contact me, but because of a miscommunication between us several years prior she had been unable to reach me again. Grace then asked Del if she would be willing to share my current address in Charlotte, and Del had promptly responded, giving her my current address.

I was speechless. All this communication had taken place totally unbeknown to me. The entire time I had been searching for my birth mother I had never once told my parents, fearing I would hurt their feelings. Ray and Del were strong, loving, and guiding lamps in our lives because they were both so steadfast, working their entire lives to provide a great life for our entire family. They had been so incredibly wonderful to me and my sisters, and I had been blessed with a childhood filled with treasured memories.

Listening to Marie relate this chain of events I was overcome with emotion, conscious that this unselfish act of love by my adoptive Mother had enabled me to reconnect with my birth mother. Del's secret gift touched me to the core. I could only imagine what she must have thought upon receiving the letter from Grace. I surmised that in her own very spiritual way, Del had decided that she would provide the information requested without telling me, and then if it was God's will, let Him make it happen.

MOTHER LOVE TRIUMPHS

Once the mystery of the six lost years had at last been explained, Marie and I proceeded to recap our lives that had ensued over the past decades, and during this lengthy conversation I learned more about my origin. Marie confirmed the information from the letter to me from Catholic Charities, stating that she had been a thirty-year-old single woman, never married, who had become pregnant, but wanted her child to be raised by a loving, two-parent family. The fact that she was 30 years old and never married was unusual at that time. A few years later, however, in September 1952, Marie had married Bill Jones, who was a few years older, and the couple made their first home in Griffith, Indiana. By then she was in her early thirties, and it was a first marriage for both, which given their ages was also unusual during the 1950s.

A few years later, Marie told me she had experienced the anguish of a miscarriage. After this loss she and Bill began contemplating adopting a child, but a year or so later, with Bill now in his early forties and Marie in her mid-thirties, they decided to simply enjoy being surrounded by both of their extended families of nieces and nephews. It was then that I realized I *was Marie's only child*, and that knowledge made this journey to reconnect even more significant for us both.

4

FACE TO FACE AT LAST

During this initial lengthy phone call with Marie, I felt I had received answers to many unresolved questions that had plagued me over the years. But now we were both anxious to meet in person. So, in late summer of 1996, I boarded a three-hour flight to Minneapolis to meet my birth mother, Marie, for the very first time. Her husband, Bill, was in a long-term care facility, and she insisted I stay with her during my visit.

As the plane touched down, I was calm yet also excited, my mind brimming with thoughts and questions. On arrival I still had a two-hour drive to her home. As I finally pulled into the driveway of her small ranch house on Hartley Lake Court NW in Brainerd, I stepped out of the car and headed up the walkway, but by that time Marie had come outside to greet me. Reunited at last, we embraced.

The next few days we spent together, sharing stories and history from the past 46 years. The first day Marie wanted me to catch up on her life and family, so she played hours of old movies of her many vacation trips to San Diego and

Disneyland in Los Angeles. Her closest sister had lived near there since the late 1940s, so she and Bill had visited her throughout the years. Marie then told me that, during her pregnancy, she had thought about the possibility of asking her sister to adopt me, but that had never materialized. The following day we took a short trip and visited a casino, but my jackpot that day was simply spending time with her.

TOUCHING MOMENTS

During our first visit in person, Marie felt the need to touch me on the shoulder or arm. She later confessed that when I was born she hesitated to hold me or touch me in the hospital. After giving birth she had remained upset about the pregnancy and even the suggestion by the birth father of having an abortion, which she refused. Her touches now were her way, after 46 years, of connecting again and embracing her son, her only child.

Marie also revealed that, in those years when I was a young boy, she often thought of me, worrying if I received enough toys for my birthday and at Christmas. I responded by telling her all about my wonderful childhood growing up in Chicago with my parents and sisters, and assured her that I had been granted her wish that I be placed in a loving, two-parent family. I emphasized that we were both blessed and fortunate in her loving, unselfish decision to give me up for adoption.

We enjoyed the remainder of our first visit together by

sharing more family stories. She told me that no one in her large family knew of her pregnancy all these years except for her mother. Her parents, Joseph and Philomena Ruesken, had both passed away in 1971. Marie also recalled that at one point during the 1980s, she often spoke with a psychic by the name of Ann Hilton, and that during one of their conversations Ann had told her, "Bill will call you." Upon hearing that, Marie was confused because her husband's name was Bill. But after I had made that initial phone call to her, Marie had realized Ann was talking about her son.

When I returned to Charlotte after our reunion, I had to admit I found it strange that we had never visited her husband Bill in the facility where he was living, nor did we see her younger brother and his family who lived in Brainerd. As it turned out, I would remain a well-kept secret for a few more years, just as I had with everyone except her mother, or so it seemed.

FAMILY TIES THAT BIND

After Marie's husband Bill passed away the following year, she moved back to the city of Lowell, Indiana, about twenty minutes south of where she had grown up. Our relationship continued to flower as I would fly back to visit her several times a year. On one of these occasions Marie planned a trip to Springfield, Illinois to visit her youngest sister, Hulda, who the family called Hermogene. She had been a Catholic nun her entire life, and at 88 was now retired from her service to the ministry.

I vividly recall the first time we met Sister Hermogene. After we finished our visit, Marie made her way back to the car, and as I walked Sister Hermogene back to the convent door, she suddenly turned to me and remarked, "I am so glad to finally meet you, Bill. I have thought about you for all these years." It was then that I realized that Sister Hermogene had also known of Marie's pregnancy and my adoption. Over the next several years, Marie and I would make the drive to Springfield to celebrate Sister Hermogene's anniversaries. It was during one of these trips where Sister Hermogene celebrated with members of her family and friends that I finally met many of Marie's brothers and their extended families.

On another trip to Indiana, Marie took me to the family cemetery and led me to the graves of her parents, where we said a short prayer together. "Mom and Dad, I finally brought my son to meet you," she added quietly. Marie and I then shared a smile and I thanked her for her prayer as we walked back to the car.

It was also during that weekend that Marie suddenly asked, "When am I going to meet my grandchildren?" She was referring to my son Ryan, now 26, and daughter Kerry, now 24. Although my children had two very loving sets of grandparents growing up, they had followed my journey to find Marie, so both understood when I asked them to join me and plan a visit to meet Marie. A few months later, the three of us flew to Indiana and enjoyed a wonderful day together with Marie. She was thrilled to get to know them, and we continued visiting her in the coming years.

In 2002, my dear mother Del suddenly passed away. She had chosen to remain living alone in Arizona over the years. Ever since my Dad's passing in 1994, I had asked her if she wanted to come live in Charlotte with me, but she insisted she was happy with her network of friends. To the day she died we never discussed my relationship with Marie, and I like to think that Del went to her grave in peace, knowing she had entrusted any reunion between Marie and me to God's will.

My sisters and me at Mom's 80th birthday, Phoenix

Mom, 24 years old

5

HOMECOMING

The year 2006 was quickly coming to an end, and I was planning to visit Marie for her 87th birthday. Over the past few years we would celebrate our birthdays together because only 17 days separated our birth dates of November 20 and December 7. I had a picture cake made to celebrate the occasion together, as I always did for these special events.

Several days after I returned to Charlotte from our birthday celebration I attempted to call Marie several times, but kept getting her voicemail. Growing concerned, I reached out to her brother, who said she had broken her leg and had undergone surgery a day earlier. I promptly made a quick trip up to Lowell to visit her in the hospital. The surgery was successful, and she would have to spend the next few months learning to walk again, but would now need the assistance of a walker. I returned to Charlotte after a few days and called her almost daily about her progress in rehabilitation.

A few months later, I was caught off guard to learn that her brother had suddenly moved Marie to an assisted living facility in Hartwell, Georgia, close to where he lived. When I called her, Marie appeared confused and less than happy with her brother's decision to sell her house and move her to Georgia. Since the facility where she was living was only a two-and-a-half-hour drive from Charlotte, I went to see her on Mother's Day in 2007. We enjoyed lunch and talked about the recent relocation decision. She had recovered well from her surgery, but privately I was not happy with the relocation decision or her new home.

A few months passed, and during one of my visits with Marie that summer I asked her if she would be interested in looking at an assisted living facility in Charlotte. She agreed, so when I returned to Charlotte, I began a search. A few days later I returned to visit her, bringing information on several facilities located only a few miles from my house. I had chosen to take this step because I was her only child, so it naturally made sense that I would be closer to her than anyone else in her family and become her caretaker.

The following week I drove Marie from Georgia to Charlotte for a short trip to check out a few facilities. Our first stop was only ten minutes from my home. We were both impressed with the staff, layout, and cleanliness of the building, and had lunch in one of the dining rooms. Before we left we thanked the director, and I was surprised when Marie said, "We don't need to visit the second location. I would enjoy being here." I told her I felt she had made a good decision, and we returned to Georgia.

Daughter Kerry, Marie, and son Ryan

The following weeks we set in motion her move to Charlotte. Fortunately, her transition went smoothly, and Marie was happily settled in her new assisted living home by the end of October 2007. I was happy to have her in Charlotte where we could visit daily. Gone at last were those long trips to Indiana.

MAKING UP FOR LOST TIME

In the years that followed Marie's move to Charlotte, I had lunches and dinners with her at the well-appointed facility where she lived. We enjoyed her favorite dessert, butter pecan ice cream, either on the front porch in warm weather or at a nearby ice cream store. At the Easter, Thanksgiving, and Christmas holidays, I would look forward to having her in my home where I would prepare some of her favorite dishes and we could relax, spending private time together. Many of those holidays Ryan, now living in Chicago, and Kerry, teaching school in Atlanta, would visit with us. Those holiday visits were special treats for Marie.

In December 2009 we celebrated Marie's 90th birthday with a lovely dinner. It was time to commemorate not just this remarkable birthday but also reflect on the last twenty years that we had been together. Yes, it had been twenty years since I placed that initial phone call that had eventually led us to this long and happy homecoming.

We sat that day and talked about how divinely guided our journey had been during those two decades, with its many twists and turns, fateful directions and decisions, and ultimately inspired determination to arrive at this point in our relationship. I truly believed that our journey was divinely guided. Marie and I seemed to have an unbreakable bond, despite our many years apart, and now had formed a deep connection. I also told Marie once again how profoundly grateful I would always be to her for making such a self-sacrificing decision to give me up for adoption so I was able to receive the blessing of a wonderful life with a loving, two-parent family.

Our journey together as mother and son continued over the next few years. A few of Marie's former neighbors in Brainerd came to visit her, and we enjoyed meeting them and sharing our life story. Ours was an amazing story that would be repeated many times through the years, not only with my friends and family, but with many of my new Ruesken cousins and family members as well.

Marie's 90th birthday

INTO THE SUNSET

Marie's years in Charlotte continued with her staying busy. The staff at the facility provided various activities from bingo games to shopping trips, and there were always planned activities, providing a warm and friendly environment for the residents. In July 2013 when returning after lunch, Marie made her usual stop in the family room to relax and enjoy conversation with friends while music from the '40s played in the background. Since her surgery to repair her broken leg, Marie had found comfort in using her walker, a common aid for people in their nineties. That day, however, she missed her chair and suddenly fell to the carpeted floor. Startled but still laughing and a bit embarrassed, she was quickly assisted back on her feet by the staff and she and her friends continued their conversation.

Weeks went by with her normal activities and routines. Soon to be 94, Marie still attended to her daily rituals without needing any assistance. She appeared strong and alert weeks after her tumble. One day as we were planning her normal wellness visit to the doctor, she complained that she couldn't get up from her chair. I suspected her fall weeks earlier had resulted in fractures in her hip, so I immediately made the decision to have her taken to the hospital.

After the x-rays were performed, a young ER doctor shared the unfortunate news, confirming my fears. He then calmly indicated that people in their nineties who suffer this type of fracture usually survive less than a year. Nonetheless, with Marie only a few months from her 94th birthday, she underwent several hours of surgery the next morning where doctors inserted three strategically placed screws in her hip. After several days of recovery and therapy in the hospital, I arranged for her next few months to be spent in a rehab facility where she would be well cared for throughout daily therapy routines.

My almost daily visits were encouraging to her as the staff attempted to make her strong enough to return to a walker, but after three challenging months it was determined she would continue her life in a wheelchair. I brought her back to her assisted living facility where she navigated her wheelchair and enjoyed being back with her friends. We celebrated her 94th birthday and Christmas that year together, birth mother and son.

The following several months, however, proved difficult for Marie. The staff at the assisted living facility could not provide the higher-level care she now required. After careful consideration, I returned her to the rehab facility where they were better equipped to meet her daily needs. Sadly, this would be her last move, as she was also now fighting a previously diagnosed issue of congestive heart failure.

I distinctly remember how the next few months Marie would be excited when I came to visit her, reaching into her pockets to show me her bingo winnings for the day — nickels, dimes, and quarters. A big smile would follow as these moments repeated themselves with each visit. My days with her would always end with my usual kiss to her forehead and soft, "I love you."

While on a short trip in October 2014, I received a phone call from the nursing facility informing me that Marie had suffered a difficult evening and they were sending her to the hospital. I immediately returned to Charlotte and within an hour was able to talk with hospital staff by phone about her condition. When they told me to bring all my legal papers with me, I knew Marie must be struggling.

On arrival at the ICU floor I found Marie weak and congested, coughing and taking oxygen. She continued in this condition for another day, and then her doctors told me her kidneys were starting to shut down. The doctor suggested placing her on a morphine drip and moved her to a private room on the same floor rather than transfer her to hospice. It was then that I knew that her remaining time with me would be short. Thankfully, her room was quiet away from the hectic ICU and as the morphine completely quieted Marie, I was greatly comforted to see her resting peacefully. Twelve hours later, my birth mother Marie, who gave me my first breath, took her last.

Marie's 94th birthday

6

REFLECTIONS ON MY JOURNEY

In the months and years that have followed Marie's passing, I find myself missing our close times together, birth mother and only child. I often reflect not only on the 25 years since I placed that fateful first phone call to her, but how I was spiritually guided and directed throughout my search. This journey was not accidental, but now has a new purpose.

I believe that I was led to create and share this journey for women and families of all ages as well as for you, my reader. I wish to continue to help others in life situations similar to the one in which Marie found herself. I hope to guide others to the realization that *adoption is an option*. Giving up a child is one of the greatest acts of love a woman and family can make together. It is a decision that can be life-giving for both child and birth mother. Marie's birth decision will always be a life-defining moment for me as I seek to support the dreams and hopes of the unborn child.

StoryTerrace®

Made in the USA
Middletown, DE
02 May 2023

29907591R00035